Impressum
Verlag: BABADADA GmbH, Nedderfeld 112 , 22529 Hamburg
Geschäftsführer / Verlagsleitung: Harald Hof
Druck: Books on Demand GmbH, In de Tarpen 42, 22848 Norderstedt

Imprint
Publisher: BABADADA GmbH, Nedderfeld 112 , 22529 Hamburg, Germany
Managing Director / Publishing direction: Harald Hof
Print: Books on Demand GmbH, In de Tarpen 42, 22848 Norderstedt

1

school

école

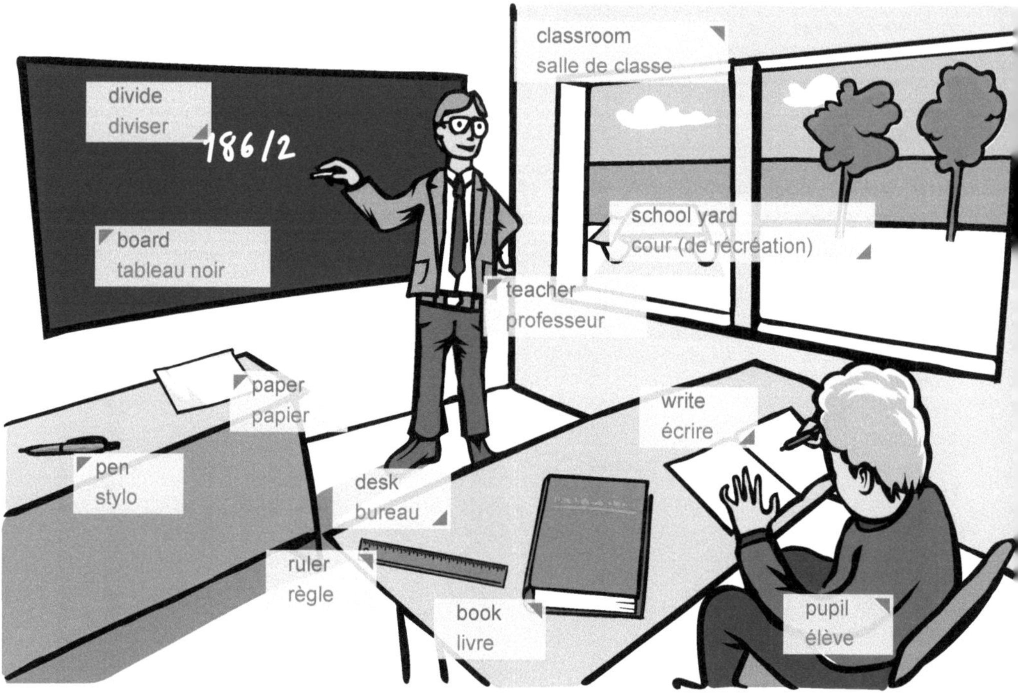
classroom
salle de classe
divide
diviser
186/2
board
tableau noir
school yard
cour (de récréation)
teacher
professeur
paper
papier
write
écrire
pen
stylo
desk
bureau
ruler
règle
book
livre
pupil
élève

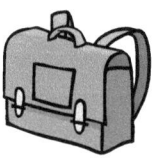

satchel

cartable

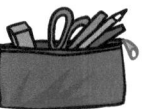

pencil case

trousse

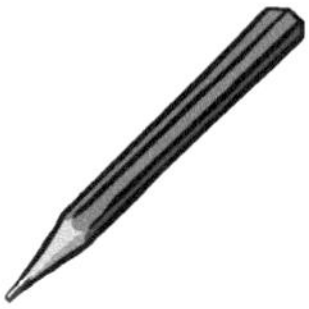

pencil

crayon

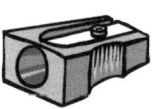

pencil sharpener

taille-crayon

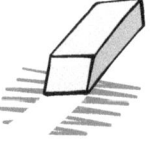

rubber

gomme

drawing pad

carnet à dessin

drawing

dessin

paintbrush

pinceau

paint box

boîte de peinture

scissors

ciseaux

glue

colle

exercise book

cahier d'exercices

homework

devoirs

number

chiffre

add

additionner

subtract

soustraire

multiply

multiplier

calculate

calculer

letter

lettre

alphabet

alphabet

word

mot

text
....
texte

read
....
lire

chalk
....
craie

lesson
....
leçon

register
....
livre de classe

exam
....
examen

certificate
....
certificat

school uniform
....
uniforme scolaire

education
....
formation

encyclopedia
....
lexique

university
....
université

microscope
....
microscope

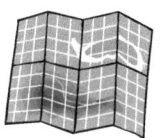

map
....
carte

paper bin
....
corbeille à papier

travel
voyage

hotel
hôtel
Grand
hostel
auberge
ROOMS
bureau de change
bureau de change
CHANGE
suitcase
valise
car
voiture

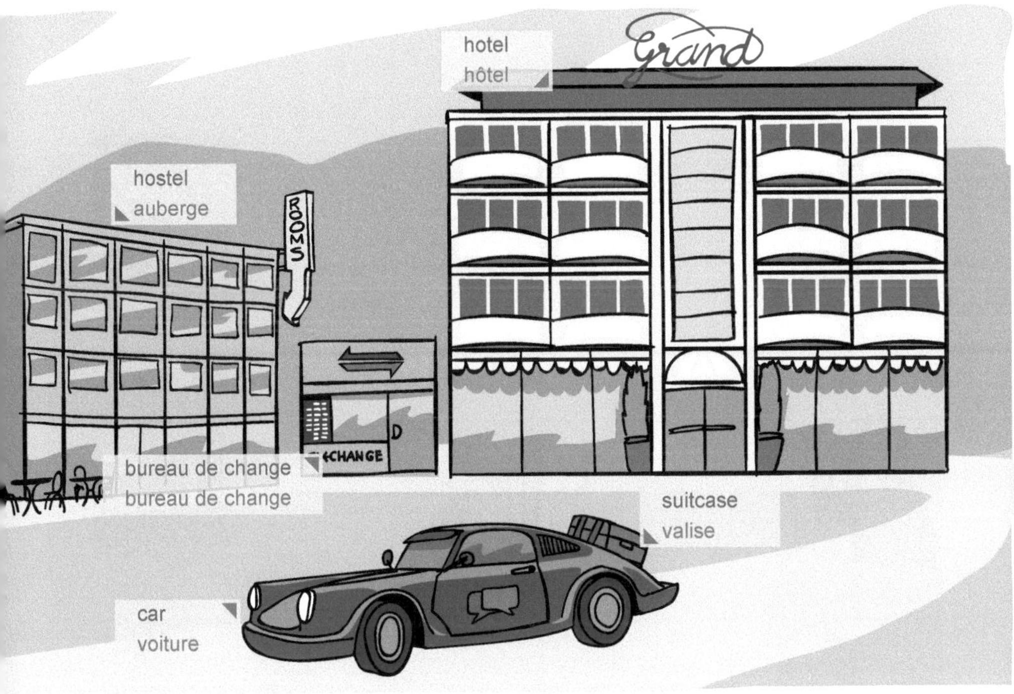

language
langue

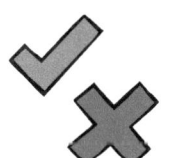

yes / no
oui / non

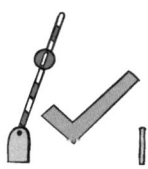

Okay
d'accord

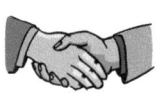

hello
Salut

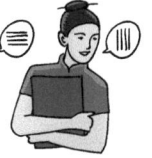

translator
interprète

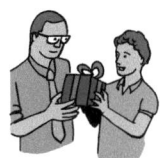

Thank you
merci

how much does ... cost?

Combien coûte...?

I do not understand

Je ne comprends pas

problem

problème

Good evening!

Bonsoir !

Good morning!

Bonjour !

Good night!

Bonne nuit !

bye bye

Au revoir

direction

direction

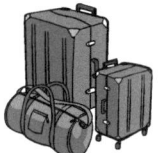

luggage

bagages

bag

sac

backpack

sac-à-dos

guest

hôte

room

pièce

sleeping bag

sac de couchage

tent

tente

travel - voyage

tourist information

office de tourisme

beach

plage

credit card

carte de crédit

breakfast

petit-déjeuner

lunch

déjeuner

dinner

dîner

ticket

billet

lift

ascenseur

stamp

timbre

border

frontière

customs

douane

embassy

ambassade

visa

visa

passport

passeport

transport
transport

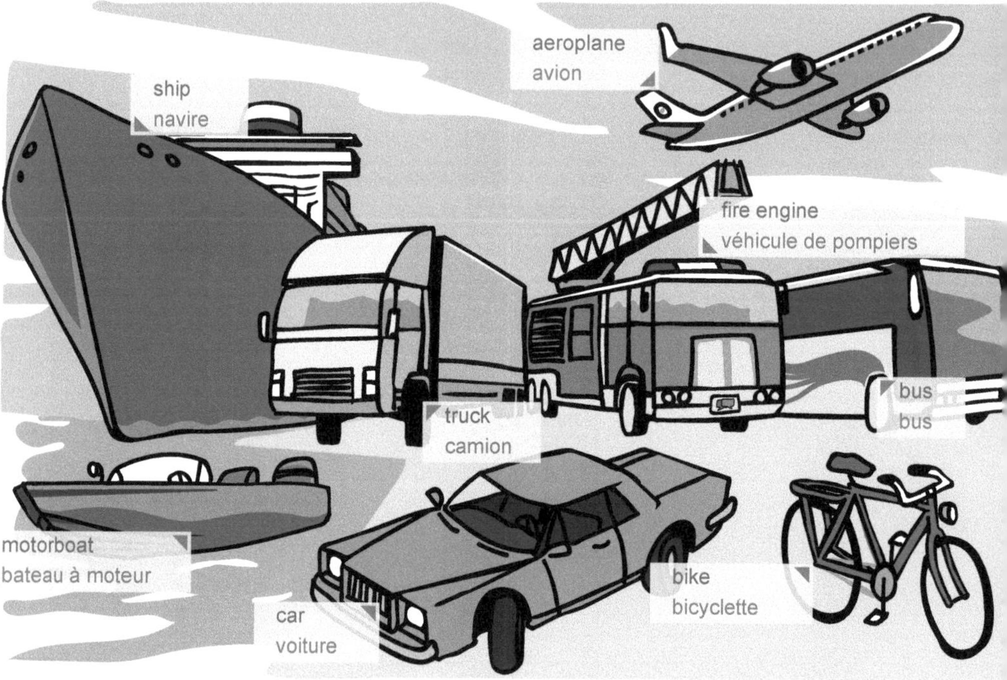
aeroplane
avion
ship
navire
fire engine
véhicule de pompiers
truck
camion
bus
bus
motorboat
bateau à moteur
bike
bicyclette
car
voiture

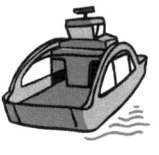

ferry

ferry

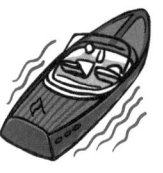

boat

barque

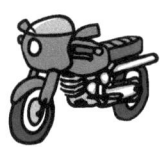

motorbike

moto

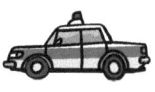

police car

voiture de police

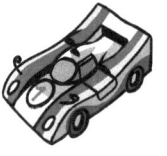

racing car

voiture de course

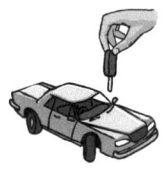

rental car

voiture de location

car sharing
auto-partage

breakdown truck
voiture de remorquage

refuse truck
benne à ordures

motor
moteur

fuel
essence

petrol station
station d'essence

traffic sign
panneau indicateur

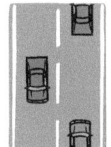

traffic
trafic

traffic jam
embouteillage

car park
parking

train station
gare

tracks
rails

train
train

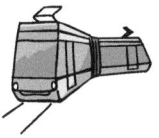

tram
tramway

carriage
wagon

helicopter

hélicoptère

airport

aéroport

tower

tour

passenger

passager

container

conteneur

carton

carton

cart

chariot

basket

corbeille

take off / land

décoller / atterrir

city

ville

village

village

city centre

centre-ville

house

maison

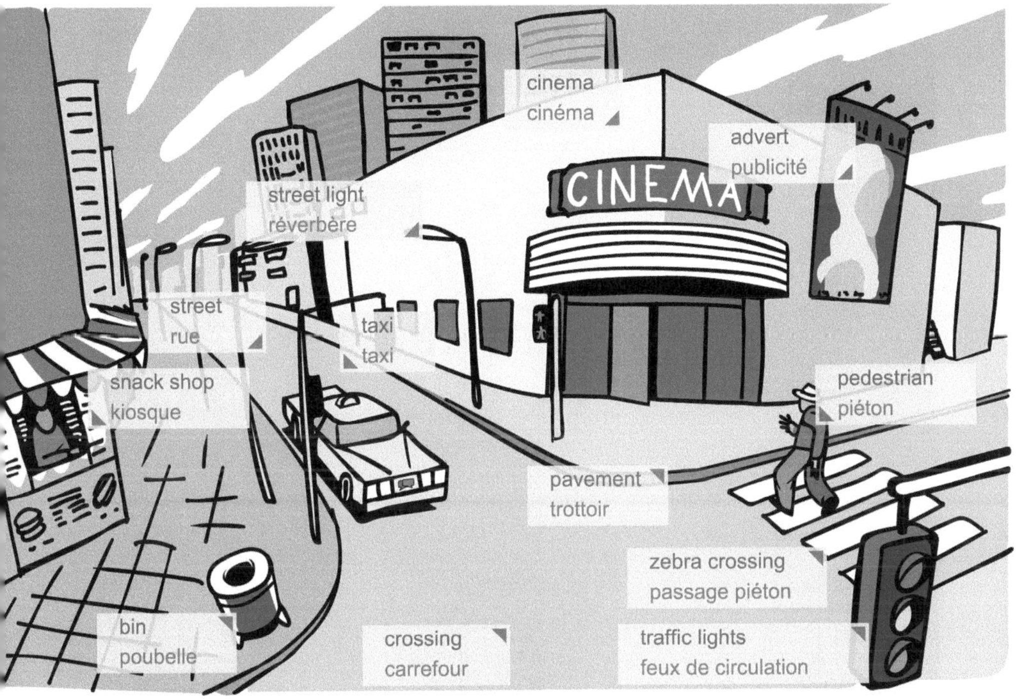

cinema
cinéma

advert
publicité

street light
réverbère

CINEMA

street
rue

taxi
taxi

snack shop
kiosque

pedestrian
piéton

pavement
trottoir

zebra crossing
passage piéton

bin
poubelle

crossing
carrefour

traffic lights
feux de circulation

hut
....
cabane

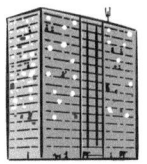

flat
....
appartement

train station
....
gare

town hall
....
mairie

museum
....
musée

school
....
école

city - ville

university
université

bank
banque

hospital
hôpital

hotel
hôtel

pharmacy
pharmacie

office
bureau

book shop
librairie

shop
magasin

florist's
fleuriste

supermarket
supermarché

market
marché

department store
grand magasin

fishmonger's
poissonnerie

shopping centre
centre commercial

harbour
port

park
parc

bench
banque

bridge
pont

stairs
escaliers

underground
métro

tunnel
tunnel

bus stop
arrêt de bus

bar
bar

restaurant
restaurant

postbox
boîte à lettres

road sign
panneau indicateur

parking meter
parcmètre

zoo
zoo

swimming pool
piscine

mosque
mosquée

farm
ferme

pollution
pollution

graveyard
cimetière

church
église

playground
aire de jeux

temple
temple

landscape
paysage

leaf / feuille

signpost / panneau indicateur

way / chemin

meadow / pré

stone / pierre

tree / arbre

hiker / randonneur

river / rivière

grass / herbe

flower / fleur

valley
vallée

hill
montagne

lake
lac

forest
forêt

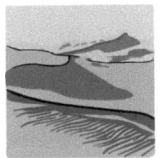
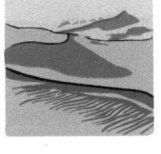

desert
désert

volcano
volcan

castle
château

rainbow
arc-en-ciel

mushroom
champignon

palm tree
palmier

mosquito
moustique

fly
mouche

ant
fourmis

bee
abeille

spider
araignée

beetle

coléoptère

frog

grenouille

squirrel

écureuil

hedgehog

hérisson

hare

lièvre

owl

chouette

bird

oiseau

swan

cygne

boar

sanglier

deer

cerf

moose

élan

dam

barrage

wind turbine

éolienne

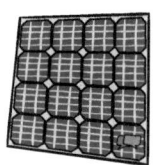

solar panel

panneau solaire

climate

climat

landscape - paysage

restaurant

restaurant

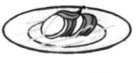

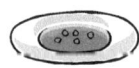

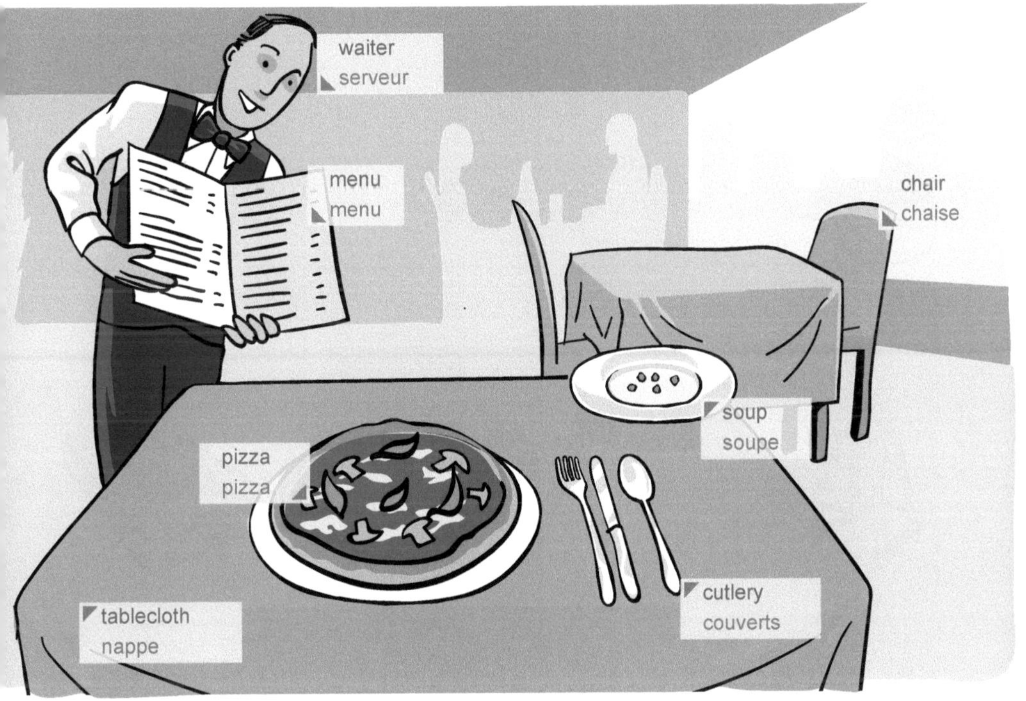
waiter
serveur
menu
menu
chair
chaise
soup
soupe
pizza
pizza
cutlery
couverts
tablecloth
nappe

starter
hors d'œuvre

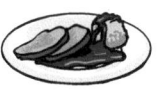

main course
plat principal

dessert
dessert

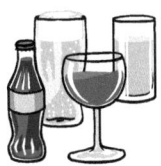

drinks
boissons

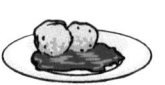

food
alimentation

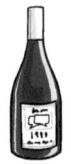

bottle
bouteille

fast food
....
fast-food

street food
....
plats à emporter

teapot
....
théière

sugar bowl
....
sucrier

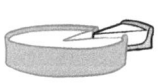

portion
....
portion

espresso machine
....
machine à expresso

high chair
....
chaise haute

bill
....
facture

tray
....
plateau

knife
....
couteau

fork
....
fourchette

spoon
....
cuillère

teaspoon
....
cuillère à thé

serviette
....
serviette

glass
....
verre

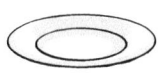

plate

assiette

soup plate

assiette à soupe

saucer

soucoupe

sauce

sauce

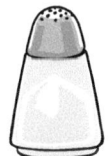

salt cellar

salière

pepper mill

moulin à poivre

vinegar

vinaigre

oil

huile

spices

épices

ketchup

ketchup

mustard

moutarde

mayonnaise

mayonnaise

supermarket
supermarché

special offer
offre promotionnelle
FOR
customer
client
dairy
produits laitiers
fruit
fruits
trolley
chariot

BUTCHERS

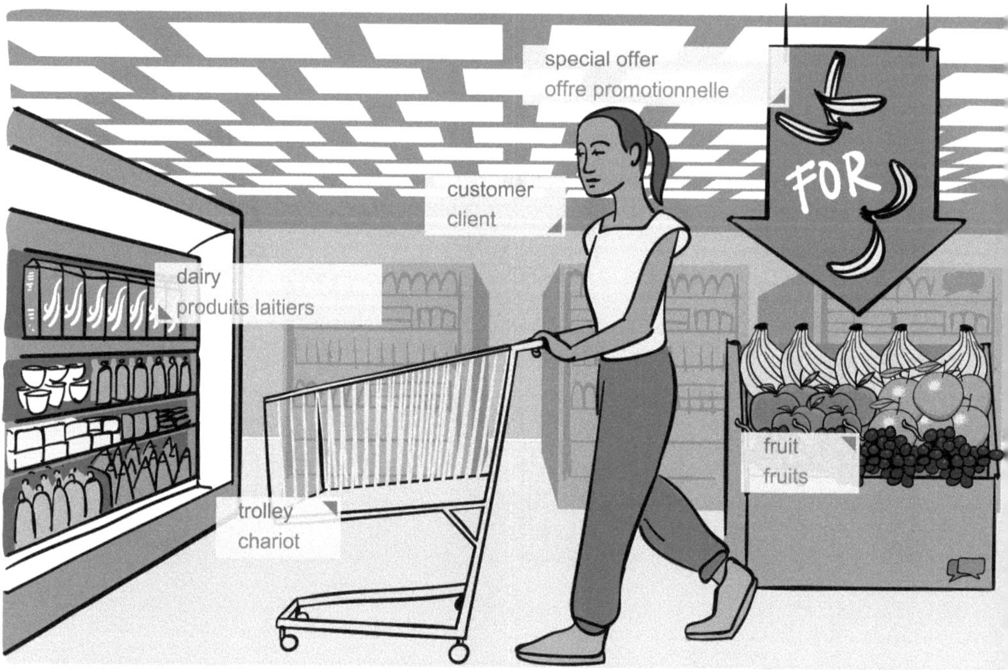

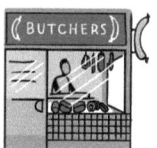

butcher´s

boucherie

BAKERY

baker´s

boulangerie

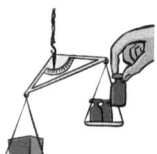

weigh

peser

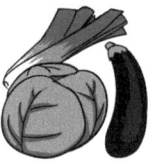

vegetables

légumes

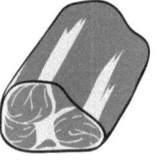

meat

viande

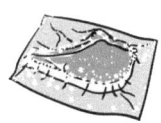

frozen food

aliments surgelés

cold meat

charcuterie

tinned food

conserves

washing powder

poudre à lessive

sweets

bonbons

household products

articles ménagers

cleaning products

détergents

salesperson

vendeuse

till

caisse

cashier

caissier

shopping list

liste d'achats

opening hours

heures d'ouverture

wallet

portefeuille

credit card

carte de crédit

bag

sac

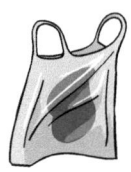

plastic bag

sac en plastique

water

eau

juice

jus de fruit

milk

lait

coke

coca

wine

vin

beer

bière

alcohol

alcool

cocoa

chocolat chaud

tea

thé

coffee

café

espresso

expresso

cappuccino

cappuccino

banana

banane

apple

pomme

orange

orange

melon

melon

lemon

citron

carrot

carotte

garlic

ail

bamboo

bambou

onion

oignon

mushroom

champignon

nuts

noisettes

noodles

pâtes

spaghetti

spaghetti

rice

riz

salad

salade

chips

pommes frites

fried potatoes

pommes de terre rôties

pizza

pizza

hamburger

hamburger

sandwich

sandwich

cutlet

escalope

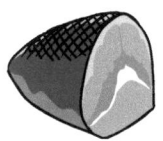

ham

jambon

salami

salami

sausage

saucisse

chicken

poulet

roast

rôti

fish

poisson

porridge oats

flocons d'avoine

muesli

muesli

cornflakes

cornflakes

flour

farine

croissant

croissant

bread roll

petits-pains

bread

pain

toast

pain grillé

biscuits

biscuits

butter

beurre

curd

le fromage blanc

cake

gâteau

egg

œuf

fried egg

œuf au plat

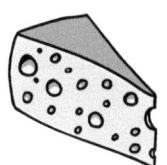

cheese

fromage

ice cream

glace

sugar

sucre

honey

miel

jam

confiture

chocolate spread

crème nougat

curry

curry

farm
ferme

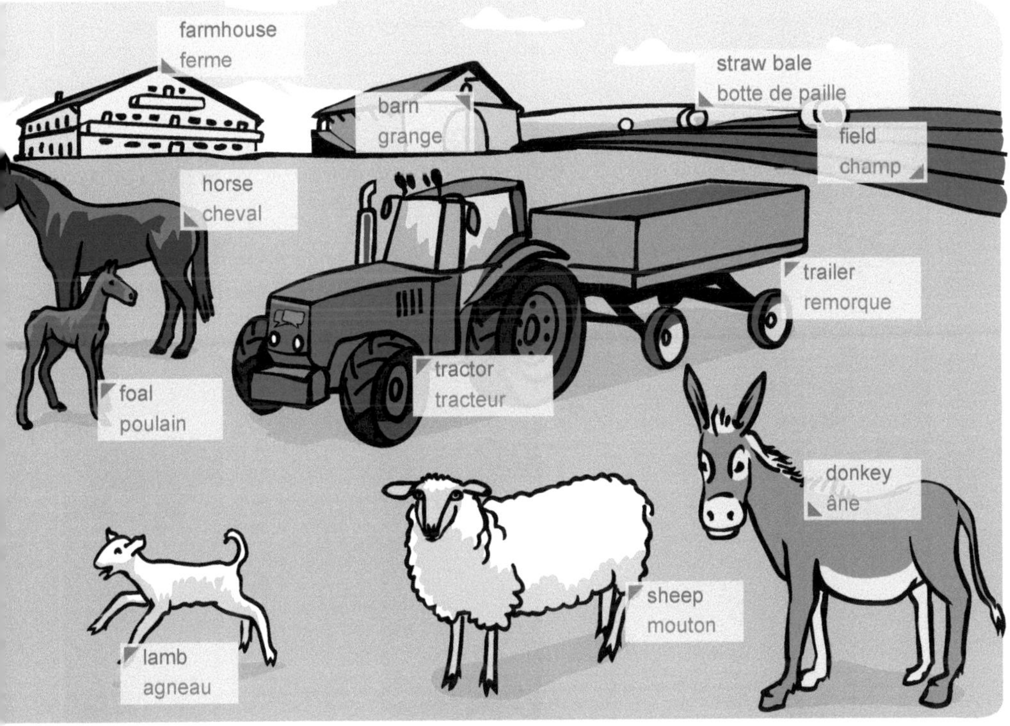
farmhouse
ferme
barn
grange
straw bale
botte de paille
field
champ
horse
cheval
trailer
remorque
tractor
tracteur
foal
poulain
donkey
âne
sheep
mouton
lamb
agneau

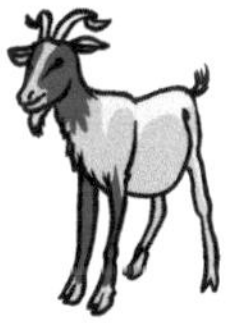

goat
chèvre

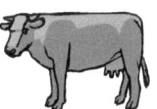

cow
vache

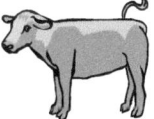

calf
veau

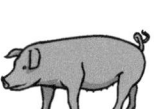

pig
porc

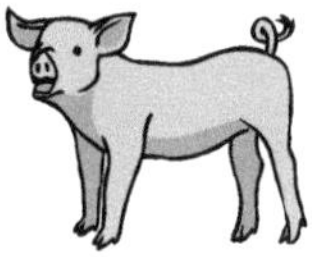

piglet
porcelet

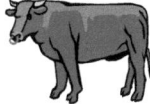

bull
taureau

goose

oie

duck

canard

chick

poussin

hen

poule

cock

coq

rat

rat

cat

chat

mouse

souris

ox

bœuf

dog

chien

doghouse

chenil

garden hose

tuyau de jardin

watering can

arrosoir

scythe

faucheuse

plough

charrue

sickle

faucille

hoe

pioche

pitchfork

fourche

axe

hache

wheelbarrow

brouette

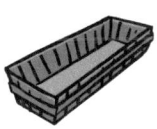

trough

cuve

milk can

pot à lait

sack

sac

fence

clôture

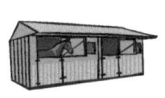

stable

étable

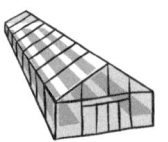

greenhouse

serre

soil

sol

seed

semences

fertilizer

engrais

combine harvester

moissonneuse-batteuse

harvest

récolter

harvest

récolte

yams

igname

wheat

blé

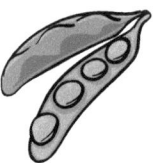

soy

soja

potato

pomme de terre

corn

maïs

rapeseed

colza

fruit tree

arbre fruitier

cassava

manioc

cereals

céréales

house

maison

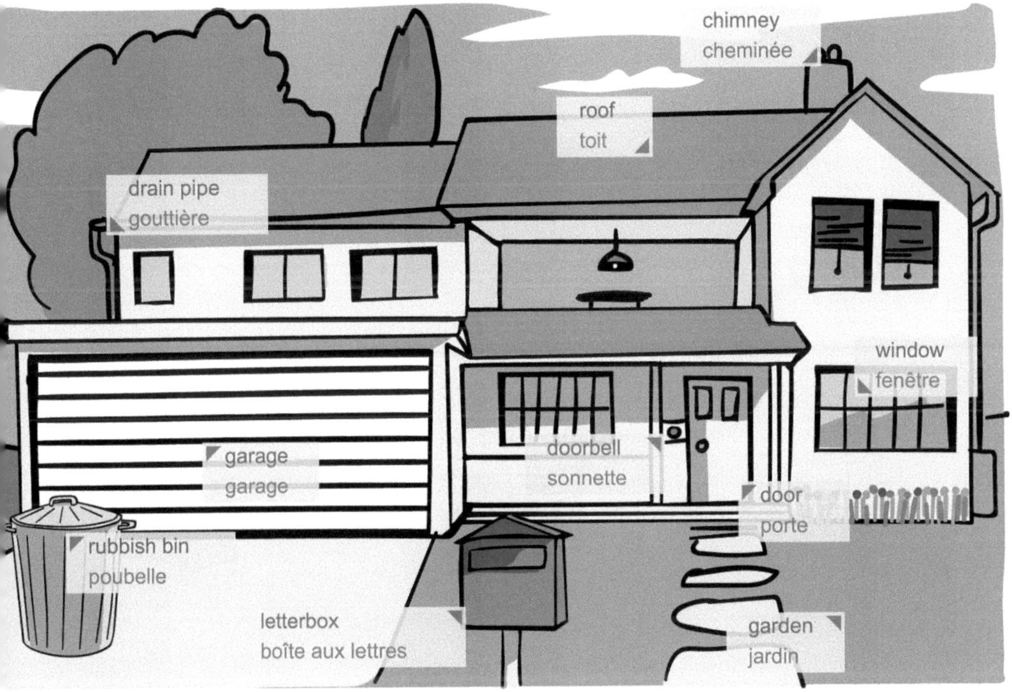
chimney
cheminée
roof
toit
drain pipe
gouttière
window
fenêtre
doorbell
sonnette
garage
garage
door
porte
rubbish bin
poubelle
letterbox
boîte aux lettres
garden
jardin

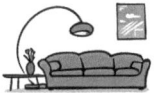

living room

salon

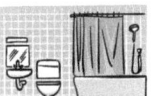

bathroom

salle de bain

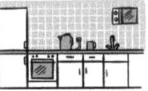

kitchen

cuisine

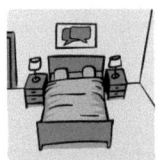

bedroom

chambre à coucher

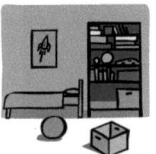

child's room

chambre d'enfant

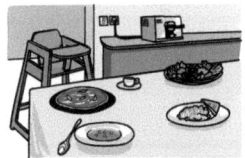

dining room

salle à manger

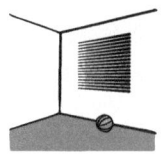

floor
....
sol

wall
....
mur

ceiling
....
plafond

cellar
....
cave

sauna
....
sauna

balcony
....
balcon

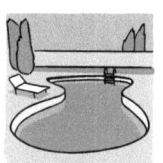

terrace
....
terrasse

pool
....
piscine

lawn mower
....
tondeuse à gazon

sheet
....
housse

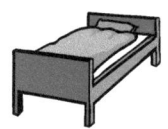

bedspread
....
couette

bed
....
lit

broom
....
balai

bucket
....
sceau

switch
....
interrupteur

house - maison

living room

salon

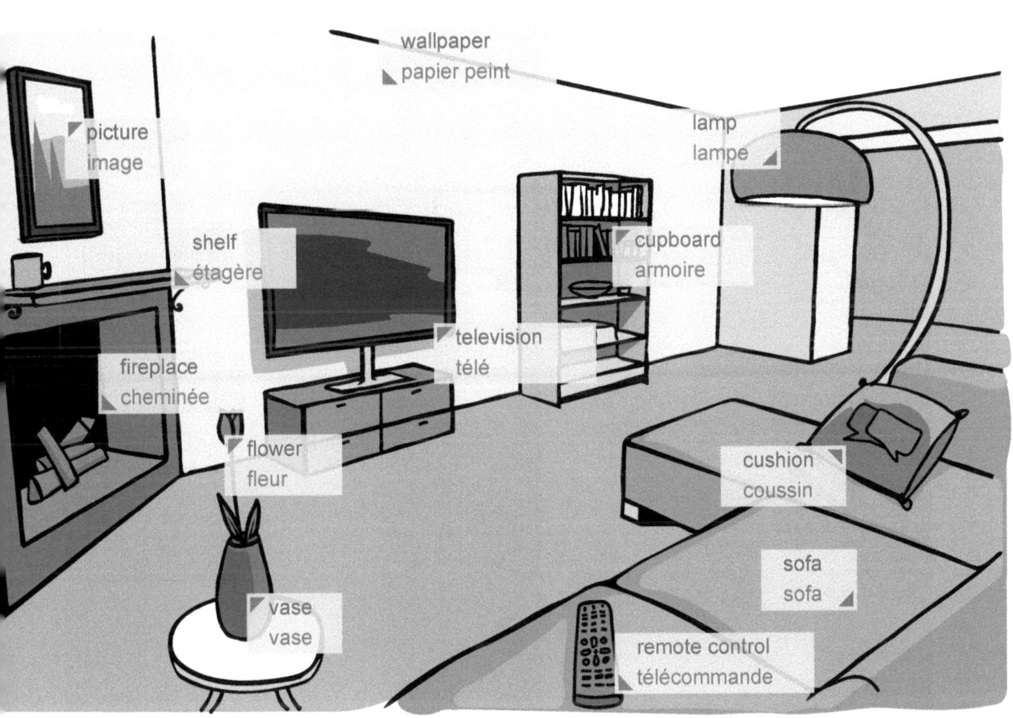

wallpaper
papier peint

picture
image

lamp
lampe

shelf
étagère

cupboard
armoire

fireplace
cheminée

television
télé

flower
fleur

cushion
coussin

sofa
sofa

vase
vase

remote control
télécommande

carpet
tapis

curtain
rideau

table
table

chair
chaise

rocking chair
chaise à bascule

armchair
fauteuil

book
livre

blanket
couverture

decoration
décoration

firewood
bois de chauffage

film
film

hi-fi equipment
chaîne hi-fi

key
clé

newspaper
journal

painting
peinture

poster
poster

radio
radio

notepad
bloc-notes

hoover
aspirateur

cactus
cactus

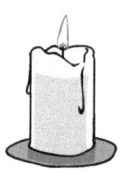

candle
bougie

kitchen
cuisine

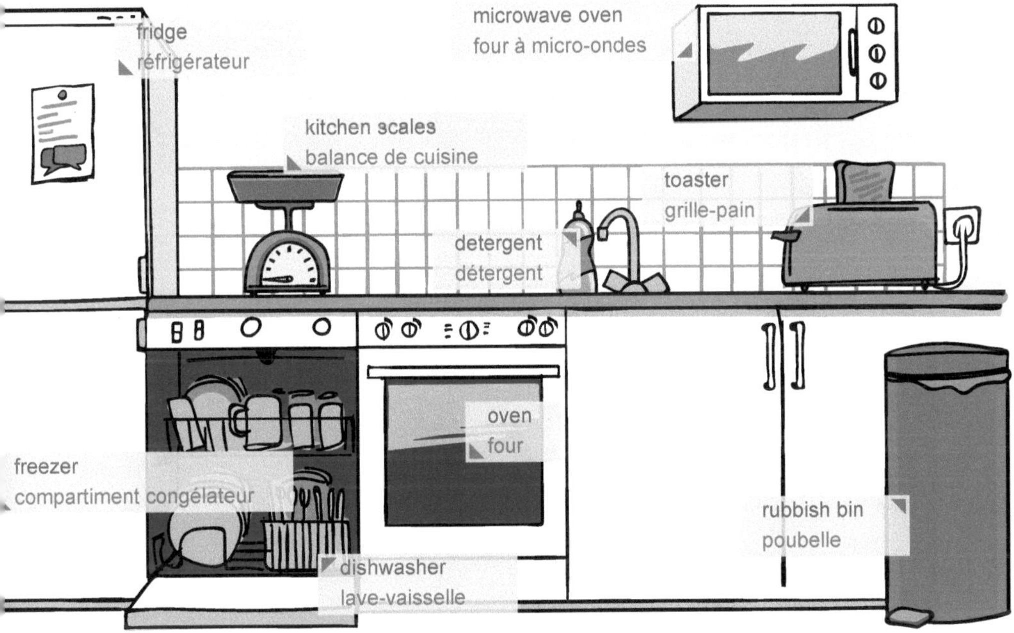

fridge
réfrigérateur
microwave oven
four à micro-ondes
kitchen scales
balance de cuisine
toaster
grille-pain
detergent
détergent
oven
four
freezer
compartiment congélateur
rubbish bin
poubelle
dishwasher
lave-vaisselle

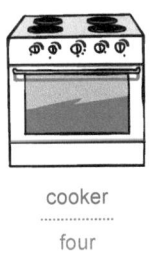

cooker

four

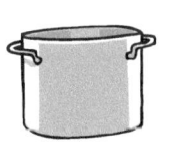

pot

casserole

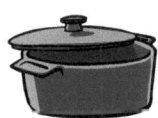

cast-iron pot

marmite

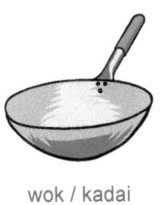

wok / kadai

wok / kadai

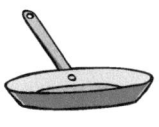

pan

poêle

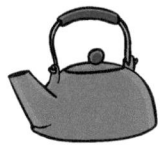

kettle

bouilloire electrique

steamer

cuiseur vapeur

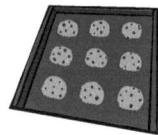

baking tray

plaque de cuisson

crockery

vaisselle

mug

gobelet

bowl

coupe

chopsticks

baguettes

ladle

louche

spatula

spatule

whisk

fouet

strainer

passoire

sieve

tamis

grater

râpe

mortar

mortier

barbecue

barbecue

open fire

cheminée

chopping board

planche à découper

rolling pin

rouleau à pâtisserie

corkscrew

tire-bouchon

can

boîte

can opener

ouvre-boîte

pot holder

maniques

sink

lavabo

brush

brosse

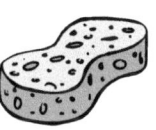

sponge

éponge

blender

mixeur

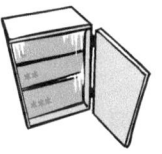

deep freezer

congélateur

baby bottle

biberon

tap

robinet

bathroom
salle de bain

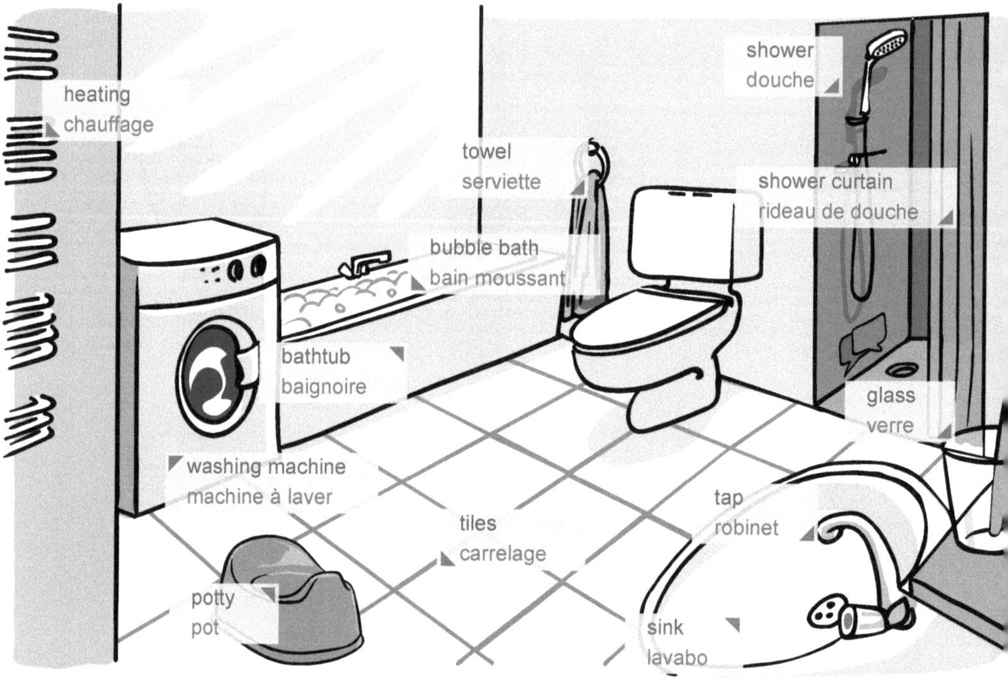

heating
chauffage
towel
serviette
shower
douche
shower curtain
rideau de douche
bubble bath
bain moussant
bathtub
baignoire
glass
verre
washing machine
machine à laver
tap
robinet
tiles
carrelage
potty
pot
sink
lavabo

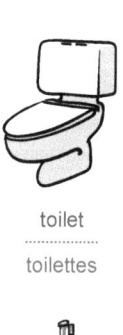

toilet

toilettes

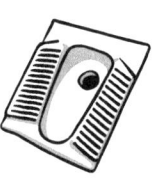

squat toilet

toilette à la turque

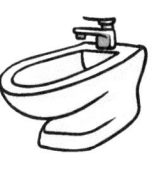

bidet

bidet

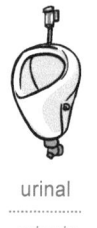

urinal

urinoir

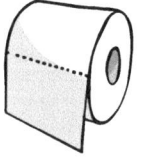

toilet paper

papier toilette

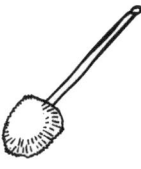

toilet brush

brosse à toilette

toothbrush
brosse à dents

toothpaste
dentifrice

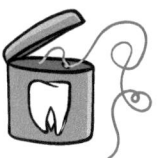

dental floss
fil dentaire

wash
laver

handheld shower
douche manuelle

douche
douche intime

basin
vasque

back brush
brosse dorsale

soap
savon

shower gel
gel douche

shampoo
shampooing

flannel
gant de toilette

drain
écoulement

cream
crème

deodorant
déodorant

mirror

miroir

hand mirror

miroir cosmétique

razor

rasoir

shaving foam

mousse à raser

aftershave

après-rasage

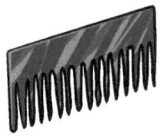

comb

peigne

brush

brosse

hair dryer

sèche-cheveux

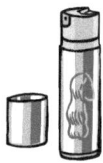

hairspray

laque pour cheveux

makeup

fond de teint

lipstick

rouge à lèvres

nail varnish

vernis à ongles

cotton wool

ouate

nail scissors

coupe-ongles

perfume

parfum

washbag

trousse de toilette

stool

tabouret

weighing scale

pèse-personne

bathrobe

peignoir

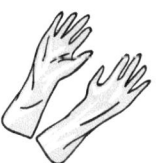

rubber gloves

gants de nettoyage

tampon

tampon

sanitary towel

serviettes hygiéniques

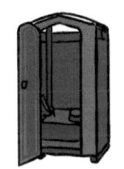

chemical toilet

toilette chimique

child's room

chambre d'enfant

alarm clock
réveil
cuddly toy
doudou
toy car
voiture jouet
rattle
hochet
doll's house
maison de poupée
present
cadeau

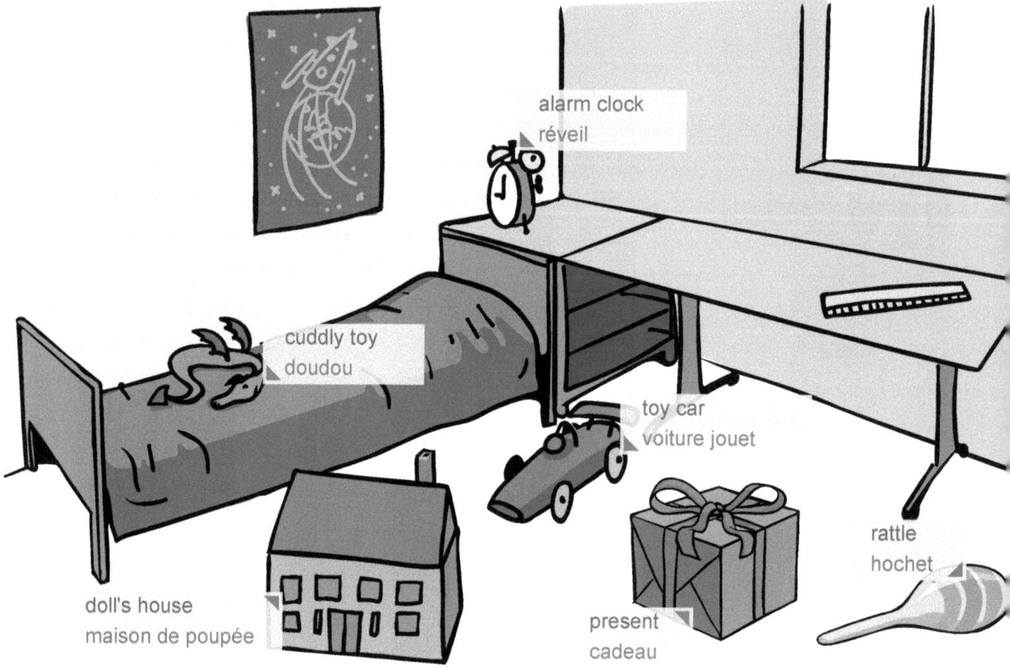

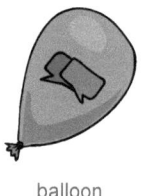

balloon

ballon

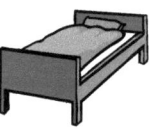

bed

lit

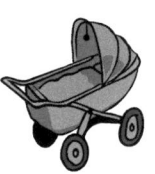

pram

poussette

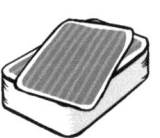

deck of cards

jeu de cartes

jigsaw

puzzle

SUPER
MEGA

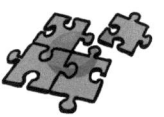

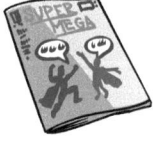

comic

bande dessinée

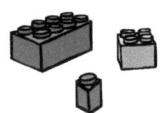

lego bricks

pièces lego

building blocks

blocs de construction

action figure

figurine

romper suit

grenouillère

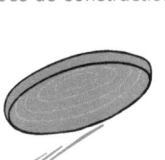

Frisbee

frisbee

mobile

mobile

board game

jeu de société

dice

dé

model train set

train miniature

dummy

sucette

party

fête

picture book

livre d'images

ball

balle

doll

poupée

play

jouer

sandpit

bac à sable

swing

balançoire

toys

jouets

video game console

console de jeu

tricycle

tricycle

teddy bear

ours en peluche

wardrobe

armoire

clothing
vêtements

socks

chaussettes

stockings

bas

tights

collant

scarf
écharpe

belt
ceinture

umbrella
parapluie

t-shirt
t-shirt

trainers
baskets

boots
bottes

slippers
pantoufles

sandals
sandales

shoes
chaussures

rubber boots
bottes de caoutchouc

underpants
sous-vêtements

bra
soutien-gorge

vest
maillot de corps

body

body

trousers

pantalon

jeans

jean

skirt

jupe

blouse

chemisier

shirt

chemise

pullover

pull

hoodie

sweat à capuche

blazer

veste

jacket

veste

coat

manteau

raincoat

imperméable

costume

costume

dress

robe

wedding dress

robe de mariée

suit

costume

nightgown

chemise de nuit

pyjamas

pyjama

sari

sari

headscarf

foulard

turban

turban

burqa

burqa

kaftan

caftan

abaya

abaya

swimsuit

maillot de bain

trunks

maillot de bain

shorts

short

tracksuit

tenue d'entraînement

apron

tablier

gloves

gants

button

bouton

glasses

lunettes

bracelet

bracelet

necklace

collier

ring

bague

earring

boucle d'oreille

cap

bonnet

coat hanger

cintre

hat

chapeau

tie

cravate

zipper

fermeture éclair

helmet

casque

braces

bretelles

school uniform

uniforme scolaire

uniform

uniforme

bib
bavoir

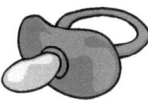

dummy
sucette

nappy
lange

office
bureau

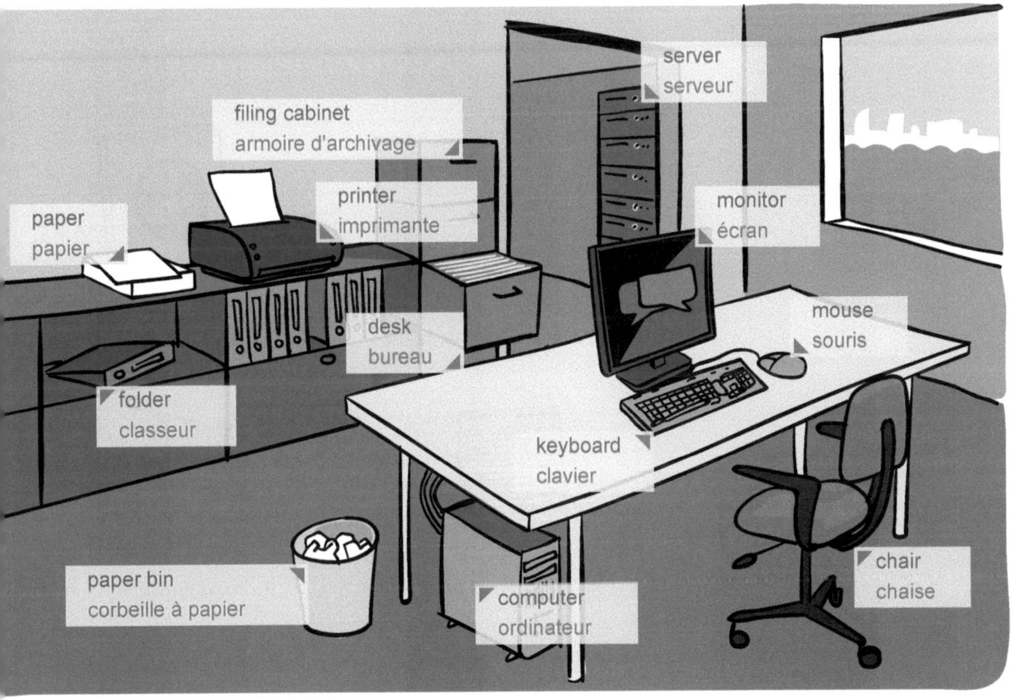

server
serveur

filing cabinet
armoire d'archivage

printer
imprimante

monitor
écran

paper
papier

mouse
souris

desk
bureau

folder
classeur

keyboard
clavier

chair
chaise

paper bin
corbeille à papier

computer
ordinateur

coffee mug
tasse de café

calculator
calculatrice

internet
internet

laptop

ordinateur portable

letter

lettre

message

message

mobile

portable

network

réseau

photocopier

photocopieuse

software

logiciel

telephone

téléphone

plug socket

prise

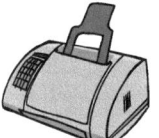

fax machine

fax

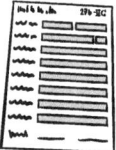

form

formulaire

document

document

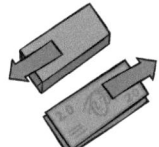

buy

acheter

pay

payer

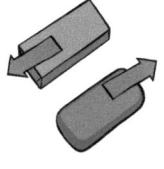

trade

faire du commerce

money

monnaie

dollar

dollar

euro

euro

yen

yen

rouble

rouble

Swiss franc

franc suisse

renminbi yuan

renminbi yuan

rupee

roupie

cashpoint

distributeur automatique

bureau de change
bureau de change

gold
or

silver
argent

oil
pétrole

energy
énergie

price
prix

contract
contrat

tax
taxe

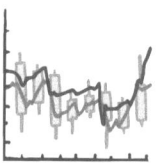

stock
action

work
travailler

employee
employé

employer
employeur

factory
usine

shop
magasin

economy - économie

occupations
professions

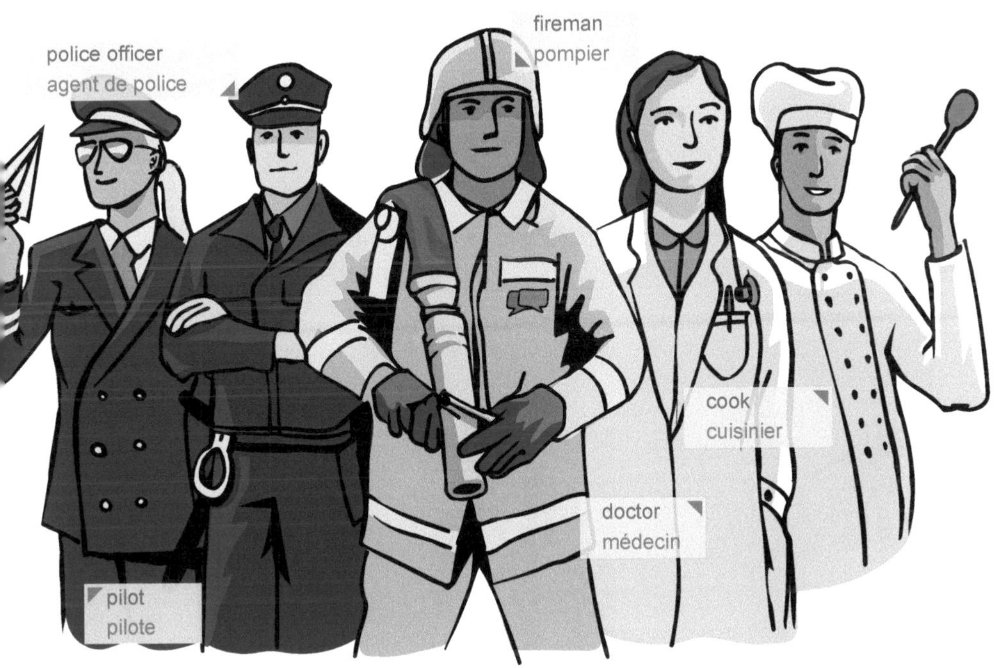
police officer
agent de police
fireman
pompier
cook
cuisinier
doctor
médecin
pilot
pilote

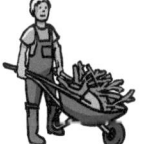

gardener

jardinier

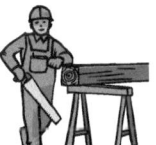

carpenter

menuisier

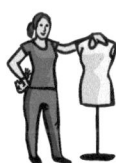

seamstress

couturière

judge

juge

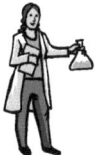

chemist

chimiste

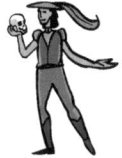

actor

acteur

bus driver

conducteur de bus

taxi driver

chauffeur de taxi

fisherman

pêcheur

cleaning lady

femme de ménage

roofer

couvreur

waiter

serveur

hunter

chasseur

painter

peintre

baker

boulanger

electrician

électricien

builder

ouvrier

engineer

ingénieur

butcher

boucher

plumber

plombier

postman

facteur

soldier

soldat

architect

architecte

cashier

caissier

florist

fleuriste

hairdresser

coiffeur

conductor

contrôleur

mechanic

mécanicien

captain

capitaine

dentist

dentiste

scientist

scientifique

rabbi

rabbin

imam

imam

monk

moine

clergyman

prêtre

tools
outils

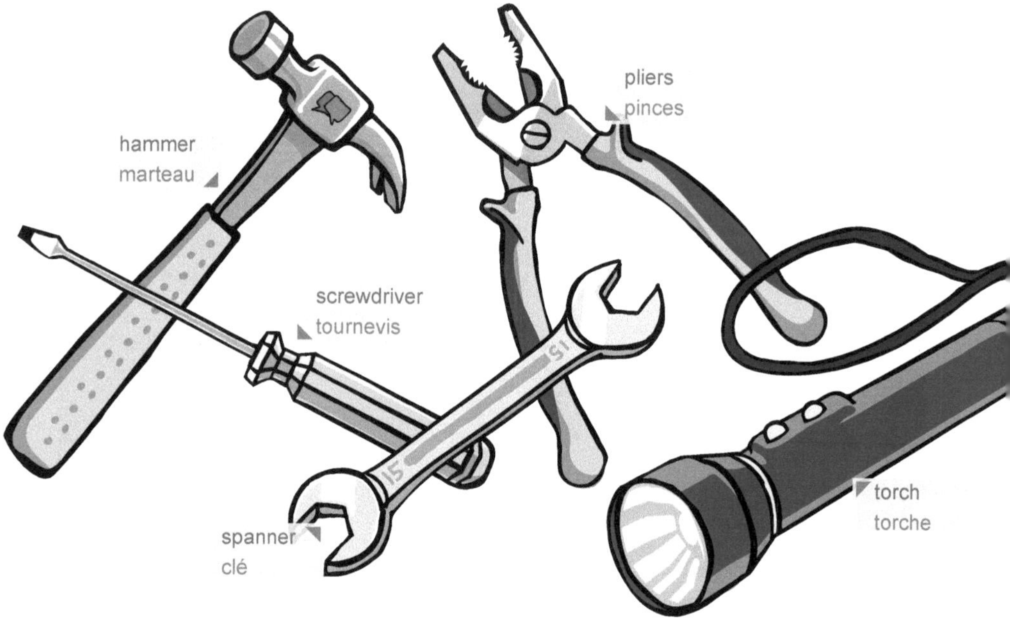

hammer
marteau

pliers
pinces

screwdriver
tournevis

spanner
clé

torch
torche

digger
pelleteuse

toolbox
boîte à outils

ladder
échelle

saw
scie

nails
clous

drill
perceuse

tools - outils

repair
réparer

shovel
pelle

Damn!
Mince !

dustpan
pelle

paint pot
pot de peinture

screws
vis

musical instruments
instruments de musique

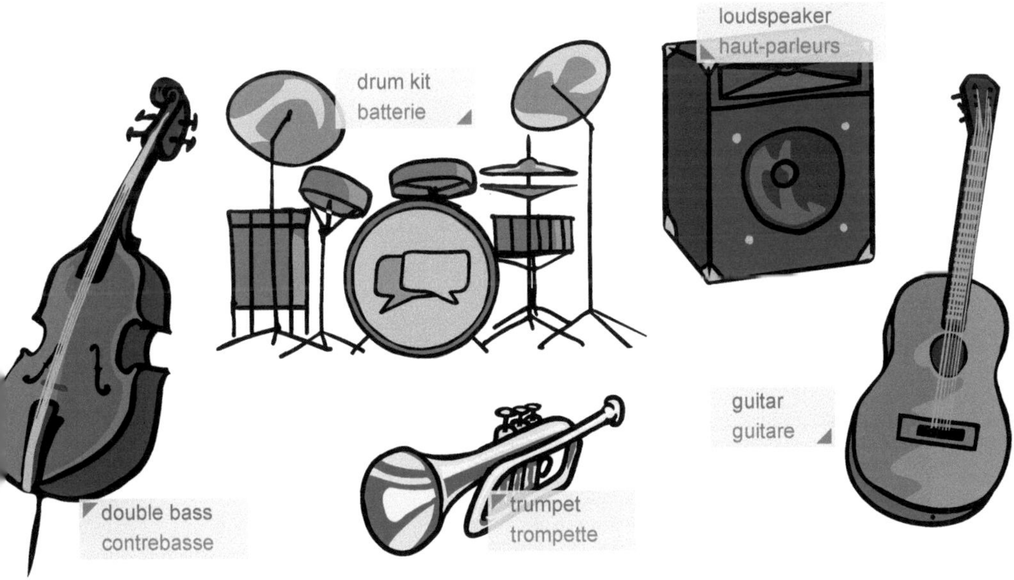

loudspeaker
haut-parleurs

drum kit
batterie

guitar
guitare

double bass
contrebasse

trumpet
trompette

piano

piano

violin

violon

bass

basse

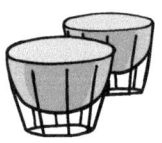

timpani

timbales

drums

tambour

keyboard

piano électrique

saxophone

saxophone

flute

flûte

microphone

microphone

musical instruments - instruments de musique

entrance
entrée

tiger
tigre

cage
cage

zebra
zèbre

animal feed
alimentation animale

panda
panda

animals

animaux

elephant

éléphant

kangaroo

kangourou

rhino

rhinocéros

gorilla

gorille

bear

ours

camel

chameau

ostrich

autruche

lion

lion

monkey

singe

flamingo

flamand rose

parrot

perroquet

polar bear

ours polaire

penguin

pingouin

shark

requin

peacock

paon

snake

serpent

crocodile

crocodile

zookeeper

gardien de zoo

seal

phoque

jaguar

jaguar

zoo - zoo

pony
poney

leopard
léopard

hippo
hippopotame

giraffe
girafe

eagle
aigle

boar
sanglier

fish
poisson

turtle
tortue

walrus
morse

fox
renard

gazelle
gazelle

American football
american Football

cycling
cyclisme

tennis
tennis

basketball
basket-ball

swimming
natation

boxing
boxe

ice hockey
hockey sur glace

football
football

badminton
badminton

athletics
athlétisme

handball
handball

skiing
ski

polo
polo

activities

activités

jump
sauter
hug
embrasser
laugh
rire
walk
marcher
sing
chanter
dream
rêver
pray
prier
kiss
faire la bise

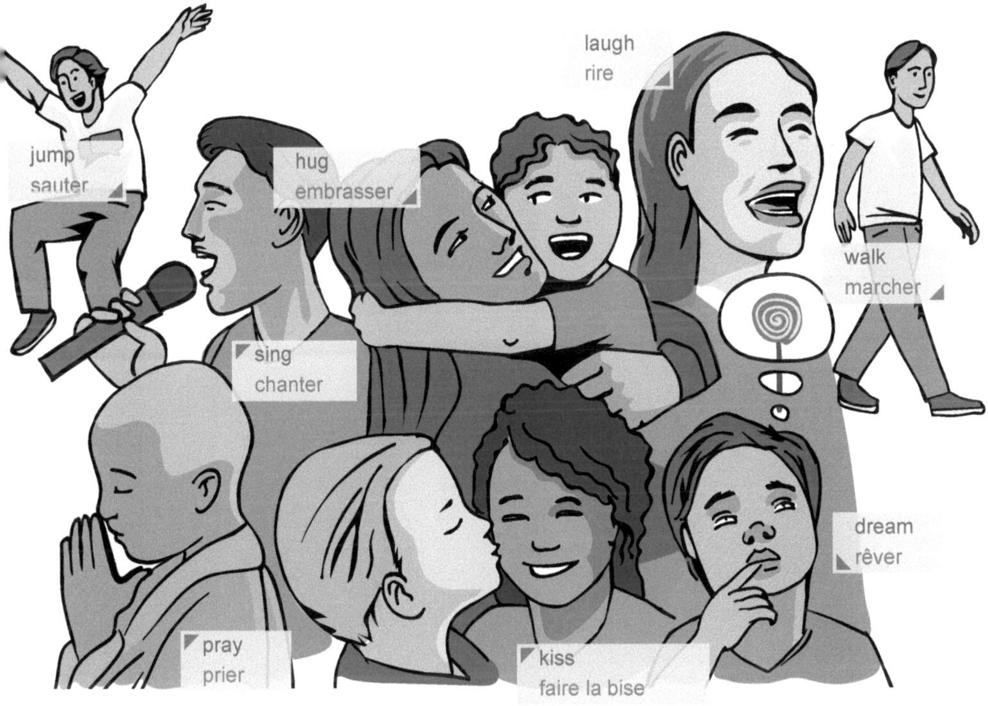

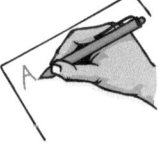

write

écrire

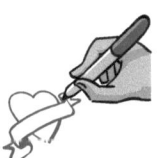

draw

dessiner

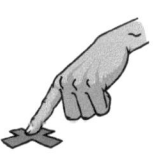

show

montrer

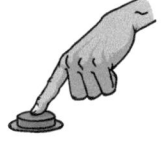

push

pousser

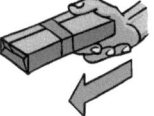

give

donner

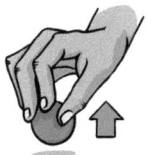

take

prendre

have
avoir

do
faire

be
être

stand
être debout

run
courir

pull
trier

throw
jeter

fall
tomber

lie
être couché

wait
attendre

carry
porter

sit
être assis

get dressed
s'habiller

sleep
dormir

wake up
se réveiller

activities - activités

look at

regarder

cry

pleurer

stroke

caresser

comb

peigner

talk

parler

understand

comprendre

ask

demander

listen

écouter

drink

boire

eat

manger

tidy up

ranger

love

aimer

cook

cuire

drive

conduire

fly

voler

sail

faire de la voile

calculate

calculer

read

lire

learn

apprendre

work

travailler

marry

se marier

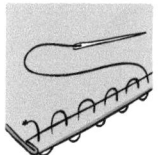

sew

coudre

brush teeth

brosser les dents

kill

tuer

smoke

fumer

send

envoyer

activities - activités

grandmother
grand-mère

grandfather
grand-père

father
père

mother
mère

baby
bébé

daughter
fille

son
fils

guest

hôte

aunt

tante

uncle

oncle

brother

frère

sister

sœur

body

corps

forehead
front
eye
œil
face
visage
chin
menton
breast
poitrine
finger
doigt
hand
main
arm
bras
shoulder
épaule
leg
jambe

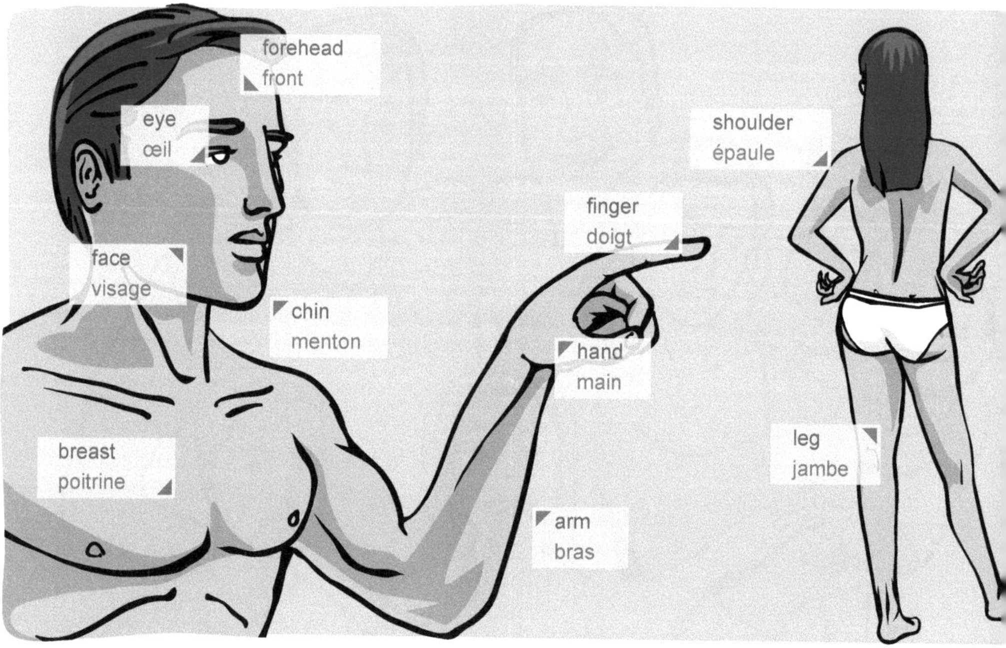

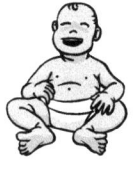

baby
bébé

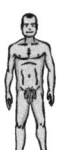

man
homme

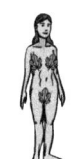

woman
femme

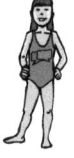

girl
fille

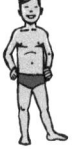

boy
garçon

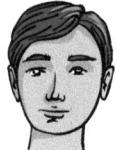

head
tête

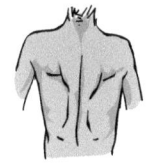

back
....
dos

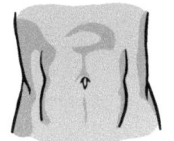

belly
....
ventre

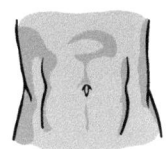

belly button
....
nombril

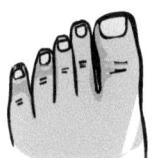

toe
....
orteil

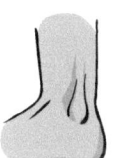

heel
....
talon

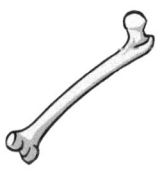

bone
....
os

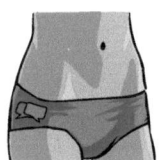

hip
....
hanche

knee
....
genou

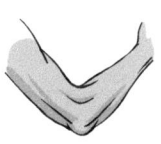

elbow
....
coude

nose
....
nez

bottom
....
fesses

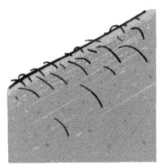

skin
....
peau

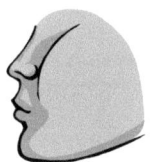

cheek
....
joue

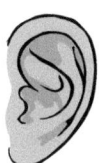

ear
....
oreille

lip
....
lèvre

body - corps

mouth

bouche

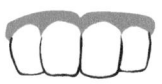

tooth

dent

tongue

langue

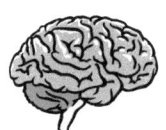

brain

cerveau

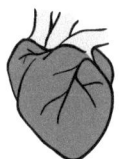

heart

cœur

muscle

muscle

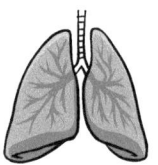

lung

poumons

liver

foie

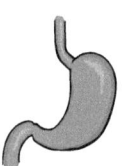

stomach

estomac

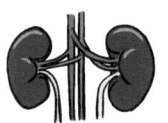

kidneys

reins

sex

rapport sexuel

condom

préservatif

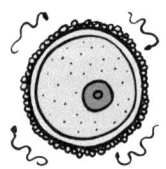

ovum

ovule

semen

sperme

pregnancy

grossesse

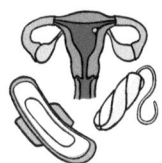

menstruation

menstruation

vagina

vagin

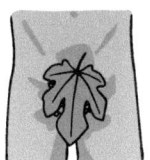

penis

pénis

eyebrow

sourcil

hair

cheveux

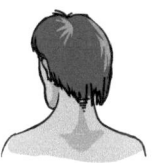

neck

cou

hospital
hôpital

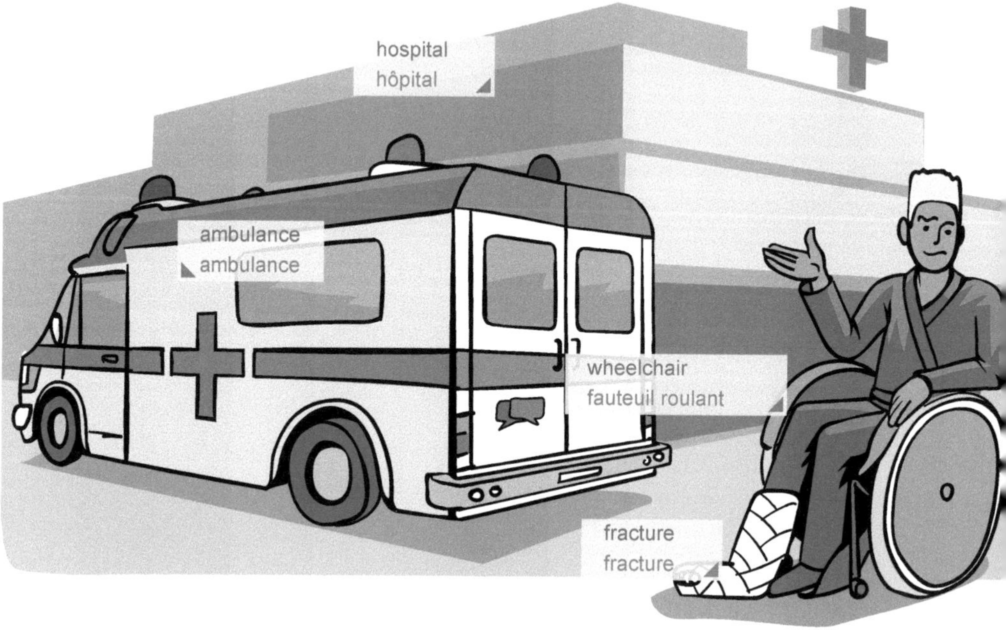

hospital
hôpital
ambulance
ambulance
wheelchair
fauteuil roulant
fracture
fracture

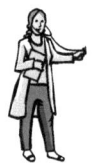

doctor

médecin

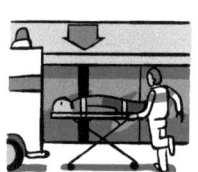

emergency room

service des urgences

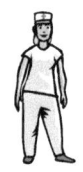

nurse

infirmière

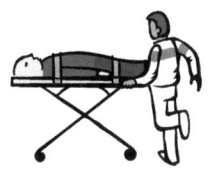

emergency

urgence

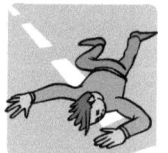

unconscious

inconscient

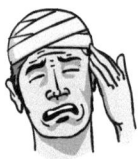

pain

douleur

injury

blessure

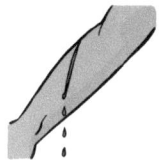

bleeding

hémorragie

heart attack

crise cardiaque

stroke

attaque cérébrale

allergy

allergie

cough

toux

fever

fièvre

flu

grippe

diarrhoea

diarrhée

headache

mal de tête

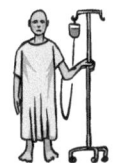

cancer

cancer

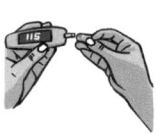

diabetes

diabète

surgeon

chirurgien

scalpel

scalpel

operation

opération

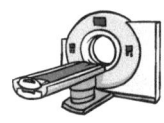

CT

CT

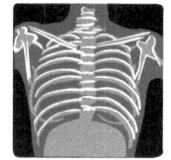

x-ray

radiographie

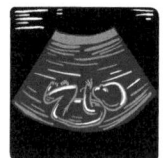

ultrasound

échographie

face mask

masque

disease

maladie

waiting room

salle d'attente

crutch

béquille

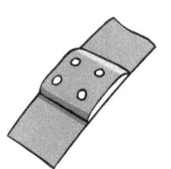

plaster

pansement

bandage

pansement

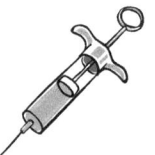

injection

injection

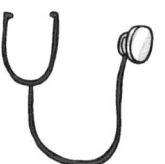

stethoscope

stéthoscope

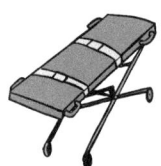

stretcher

brancard

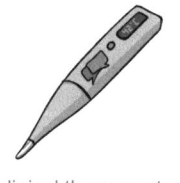

clinical thermometer

thermomètre

birth

accouchement

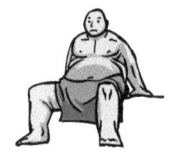

overweight

surcharge pondérale

hearing aid

appareil auditif

disinfectant

désinfectant

infection

infection

virus

virus

HIV / AIDS

VIH / sida

medicine

médicament

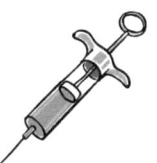

vaccination

vaccination

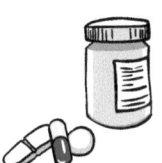

tablets

comprimés

pill

pilule

emergency call

appel d'urgence

blood pressure monitor

tensiomètre

sick / healthy

malade / sain

Help!

Au secours !

alarm

alarme

assault

assaut

attack

attaque

danger

danger

emergency exit

sortie de secours

Fire!

Au feu!

fire extinguisher

extincteur

accident

accident

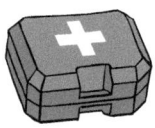

first-aid kit

trousse de premier secours

SOS

SOS

police

police

Europe

Europe

North America

Amérique du Nord

South America

Amérique du Sud

Africa

Afrique

Asia

Asie

Australia

Australie

Atlantic

Océan atlantique

Pacific

Océan pacifique

Indian Ocean

Océan indien

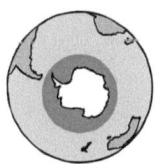

Antarctic Ocean

Océan antarctique

Arctic Ocean

Océan arctique

North Pole

pôle nord

South Pole
pôle sud

Antarctica
Antarctique

Earth
terre

land
pays

sea
mer

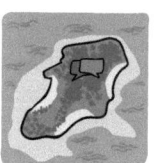

island
île

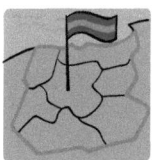

nation
nation

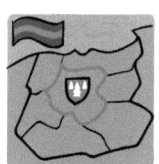

state
état

clock face
cadran

hour hand
aiguille des heures

minute hand
aiguille des minutes

second hand
aiguille des secondes

What time is it?
Quelle heure est-il ?

day
jour

time
temps

now
maintenant

digital watch
montre digitale

minute
minute

hour
heure

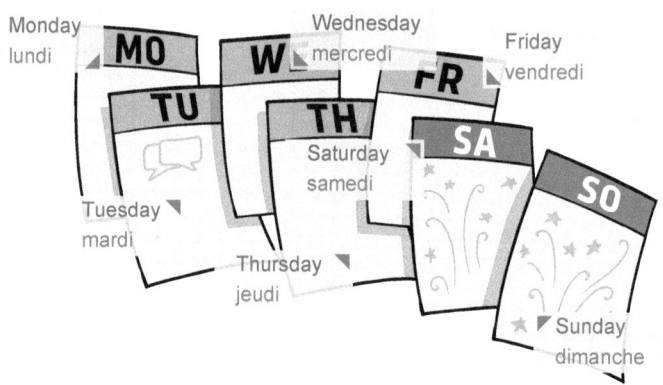

Monday / lundi
Tuesday / mardi
Wednesday / mercredi
Thursday / jeudi
Friday / vendredi
Saturday / samedi
Sunday / dimanche

yesterday

hier

today

aujourd'hui

tomorrow

demain

morning

matin

noon

midi

evening

soir

MO	TU	WE	TH	FR	SA	SU
1	2	3	4	5	6	7
8	9	10	11	12	13	14
15	16	17	18	19	20	21
22	23	24	25	26	27	28
29	30	31	1	2	3	4

business days

jours ouvrables

MO	TU	WE	TH	FR	SA	SU
1	2	3	4	5	6	7
8	9	10	11	12	13	14
15	16	17	18	19	20	21
22	23	24	25	26	27	28
29	30	31	1	2	3	4

weekend

week-end

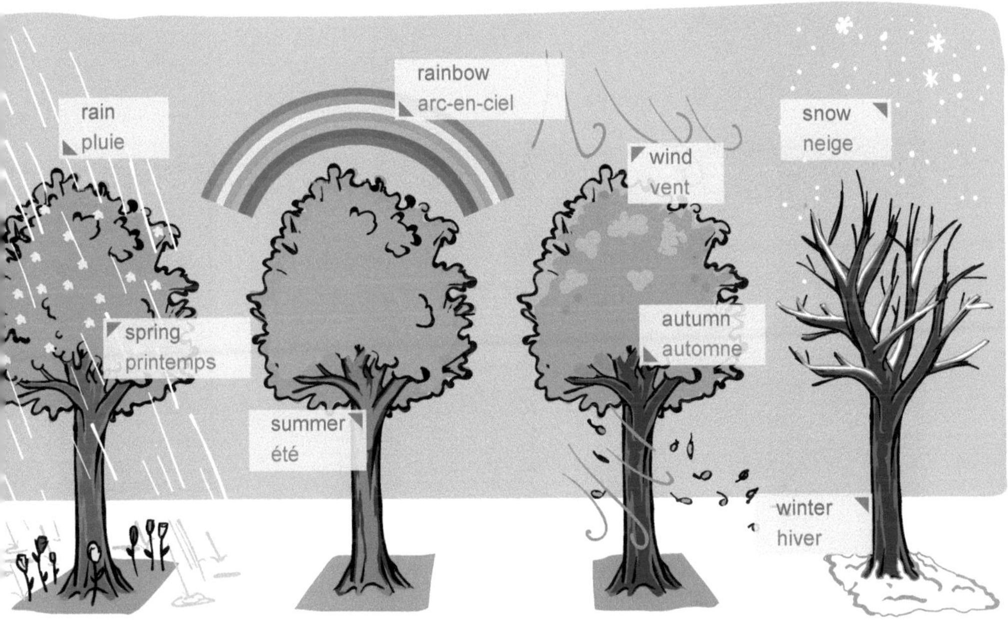

rain
pluie
rainbow
arc-en-ciel
wind
vent
snow
neige
spring
printemps
autumn
automne
summer
été
winter
hiver

4.APRIL 11°
5.APRIL 4°
6.APRIL 13°
7.APRIL 8°
8.APRIL 10°

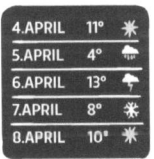

weather forecast

météo

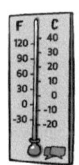

thermometer

thermomètre

sunshine

lumière du soleil

cloud

nuage

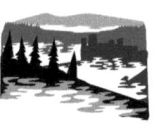

fog

brouillard

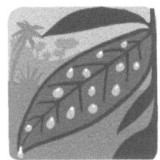

humidity

humidité

lightning

foudre

thunder

tonnerre

storm

tempête

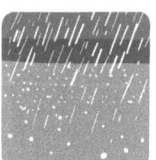

hail

grêle

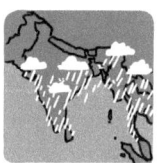

monsoon

mousson

flood

inondation

ice

glace

January

janvier

February

février

March

mars

April

avril

May

mai

June

juin

July

juillet

August

août

year - année

September
....
septembre

October
....
octobre

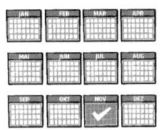

November
....
novembre

December
....
décembre

circle
....
cercle

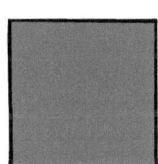

square
....
carré

rectangle
....
rectangle

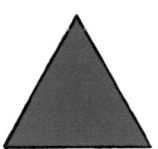

triangle
....
triangle

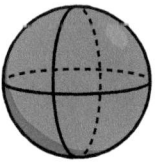

sphere
....
sphère

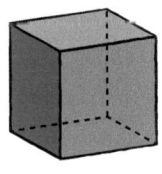

cube
....
cube

colours
couleurs

white
blanc

yellow
jaune

orange
orange

pink
rose

red
rouge

purple
violet

blue
bleu

green
vert

brown
marron

grey
gris

black
noir

a lot / a little

beaucoup / peu

angry / calm

fâché / calme

beautiful / ugly

joli / laid

beginning / end

début / fin

big / small

grand / petit

bright / dark

clair / obscure

brother / sister

frère / soeur

clean / dirty

propre / sale

complete / incomplete

complet / incomplet

day / night

jour / nuit

dead / alive

mort / vivant

wide / narrow

large / étroit

edible / inedible

comestible / incomestible

evil / nice

méchant / gentil

excited / bored

excité / ennuyé

fat / thin

gros / mince

first / last

premier / dernier

friend / enemy

ami / ennemi

full / empty

plein / vide

hard / soft

dur / souple

heavy / light

lourd / léger

hunger / thirst

faim / soif

sick / healthy

malade / sain

illegal / legal

illégal / légal

intelligent / stupid

intelligent / stupide

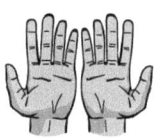

left / right

gauche / droite

near / far

proche / loin

new / used

nouveau / usé

nothing / something

rien / quelque chose

old / young

vieux / jeune

on / off

marche / arrêt

open / closed

ouvert / fermé

quiet / loud

faible / fort

rich / poor

riche / pauvre

right / wrong

correct / incorrect

rough / smooth

rugueux / lisse

sad / happy

triste / heureux

short / long

court / long

slow / fast

lent / rapide

wet / dry

mouillé / sec

warm / cool

chaud / froid

war / peace

guerre / paix

0

zero

zéro

1

one

un / une

2

two

deux

3

three

trois

4

four

quatre

5

five

cinq

6

six

six

7

seven

sept

8

eight

huit

9

nine

neuf

10

ten

dix

11

eleven

onze

12

twelve

douze

13

thirteen

treize

14

fourteen

quatorze

15

fifteen

quinze

16

sixteen

seize

17

seventeen

dix-sept

18

eighteen

dix-huit

19

nineteen

dix-neuf

20

twenty

vingt

100

hundred

cent

1.000

thousand

mille

1.000.000

million

million

English
....
anglais

American English
....
anglais américain

Mandarin Chinese
....
chinois mandarin

Hindi
....
hindi

Spanish
....
espagnol

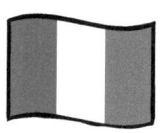

French
....
français

Arabic
....
arabe

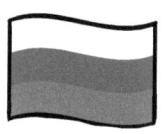

Russian
....
russe

Portuguese
....
portugais

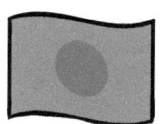

Bengali
....
bengali

German
....
allemand

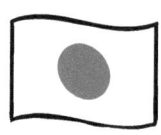

Japanese
....
japonais

I

je

you

tu

he / she / it

il / elle / ce, c', cela

we

nous

you

vous

they

ils / elles

who?

Qui ?

what?

Quoi ?

how?

Comment ?

where?

Où ?

when?

Quand ?

name

nom

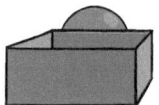

behind

derrière

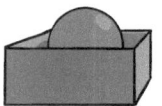

in

dans

in front of

devant

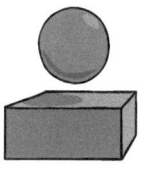

over

au-dessus

on

sur

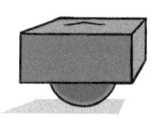

under

en-dessous

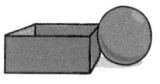

beside

à côté de

between

entre

place

lieu